Sisters of Notre Dame (Cincinatti Ohio)

May Blossoms

a collection of hymns to the Blessed Virgin

Sisters of Notre Dame (Cincinatti Ohio)

May Blossoms
a collection of hymns to the Blessed Virgin

ISBN/EAN: 9783337089580

Printed in Europe, USA, Canada, Australia, Japan

Cover: Foto ©Lupo / pixelio.de

More available books at **www.hansebooks.com**

May Blossoms

A COLLECTION OF

HYMNS TO THE BLESSED VIRGIN.

COMPILED AND ARRANGED BY THE

SISTERS OF NOTRE DAME,

CINCINNATI, OHIO.

BOSTON:
OLIVER DITSON COMPANY.

NEW YORK: CHICAGO: PHILA: BOSTON:
C. H. Ditson & Co. Lyon & Healy. J. E. Ditson & Co. John C. Haynes & Co.

DEDICATORY.

TO MARY,

The Mistress of our Hearts, the Theme of all our Lays.

Queen of our songs! their sweetest notes must fall
But as the echo of bright hopes that yearningly
Soar to that sphere where Love, transcending all,
Breaks forth, unhushed in Heaven-born anthems burningly.
Queen of the flowers! these breathing buds to thee
We bring, all trembling in their lowliness:
Their fairest charm—thy spotless purity;
Their perfume—thy unshadowed holiness.
Mother of God! we lay them at thy feet,
Song-wreaths in Winter-time still blooming vernally.
Oh! may each soul its pure thought-blossom meet
On golden seas where song-waves break eternally,
"MAY BLOSSOMS" heart-carols echoing on that shore
Where ceaseless chimes are pealing evermore.

No. 1. MARY QUEEN OF MY SOUL.

Words by Mrs. MONROE.   Solo and 2 part chorus.   Music by WOLLASTON.

SOLO.

1. O Moth-er loved, whose starlike eyes Are all the light I seek, Look
2. Be-hold where kings and shepherds meet Beneath that star di-vine, I
3. On E-gypt's flight let me attend, And by thy toilsome way Thy
4. On Calvary's dark and fear-ful height A-gain I kneel by thee, A-

1. from thy home be-yond the skies And hear me whilst I speak, And
2. bow me at thy sa-cred feet And give this heart of mine, This
3. meek en-dur-ance to me lend And ev-er for me pray, And
4. -mid the an-guish of that night, Lov'd mother pray for me, Oh

CHORUS.   espress rit.

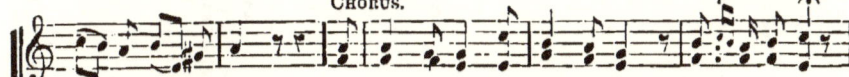

1. hear me whilst I speak.   O take me 'neath thy loved control, Queen of my soul,
2. wayward heart of mine.   O take me 'neath thy loved control, &c.
3. ev-er for me pray.   I fly to seek thy loved control, &c.
4. Ma-ry pray for me.   Thy bitter grief knew no control, &c.

Andante espress.

Ma-ry,   Ma-ry,   Queen of my soul,   Ma-ry,   Ma-ry,   Queen of my soul.

5 By all thy sorrows once endured,
    The bliss that now is given,
Oh! let my earnest cry be heard
    By thee blest Queen of Heaven,
    By thee blest Queen of Heaven,
Cho.—Bright angels bow to thy control,
    Queen of my soul,
    ||: Mary, Mary. Queen of my soul. :||

6 What dazzling glories now surround
    Thy home beyond the sky,
E'en there thy faithful child is found,
    To kneel with suppliant cry,
    To kneel with suppliant cry.
Cho.—Oh take me 'neath thy loved control,
    Queen of my soul,
    ||: Mary, Mary, Queen of my soul :||

*These Hymns are also published with Piano accompaniment, under the title of
"May Chimes." Price, $1.25.*

No. 2. CONSECRATION TO MARY.

Solo and Chorus.

Words AVE MARIA.   Music by C. SCHUBERT.

Solo.

1. My Moth-er dear,..... my Queen di - vine,..... My
2. By all the love...... that made Him thine,.... To

heart, my soul, my life are thine ;.... All that I am,...... or e'er will
ev - 'ry suppliant at thy shrine,... Queen Mother of........ our fallen

be,........ For once, for all,...... I give to thee, And, through thy
race,...... In life, in death,... impart this grace, From hour to

ritard. rall.

sin - less bands, to Him, Thy son. whose heart for us was riv'n......
hour,.... to love thee more, Till heav'n is won, and ex - ile o'er.......

Chorus.

1st. V. *Religioso con espress.*

O   sweet Madon - na, hear   me, From this dark world of woes,   Thy

2d. V.

fee - ble child im - plores   thee, Thy.... lov - ing

heart,   thy heart...........   thy heart un-close.

No. 3. EVE OF MAY

DUET OR 2 PART CHORUS AND SOLO.

Words by S. N. D.   Music by L. LAMBILLOTTE.

Come gath - er round the al - tar, To Ma - ry each heart of - fer, While glad-ly as our Queen to-day, We crown her with the op'n-ing May, Come, haste, each heart.... at her loved feet now lay,.... Come, haste.... each heart...... at her loved feet now lay...................

SOLO· *Piu lento.*

1. The ice bonds of win - ter are bro - ken, A - gain we hail sweet
2. See na - ture has donned all her gay - est, To greet our Moth - er
3. The soft blushing ro - ses are tremb - ling, With long - ings to be
4. Then Ma - ry our Queen and our Moth - er, Ac - cept the hearts we

ritard.

1. May,...... And Ma - ry, bless'd Ma - ry we're crown - ing As our
2. Queen,.... And flow - ers the brightest and fair - - est, Ma - ry's
3. placed,.... On our Mother's al - tar im - pa - tient For
4. bring..... And all through life's stormi - est weath - er, Grant

D.S.CHORUS. :8:

1. cho - sen Queen to - day.....
2. chil - dren for her glean...
3. her their soft fragrance to waste...
4. that to thee we may cling....

Come

No. 4. THE STORM.

DUET OR 2 PART CHORUS AND SOLO.

Words by Pupil of S. N. D.   Music by L. LAMBILLOTTE.

DUET. *ff*

1. The   storm   is   wild-ly   'rag - ing,   Moth - er
2. Bright star   in   beau-ty   beam - ing,   Shine o'er

haste, moth-er haste   to   our   aid,   Fierce   winds   in   war en-
us, shine o'er us   thro' the   dark,   Thy   light   all   spark-ling,

dim.   *p*   *ri - tar - do.*

-gag - ing,   Calm the   storm, calm the storm, peer - less   maid.
gleam-ing,   Guide a - right, guide a-right   our   frail   bark.

Solo. *Espress.*

1. Guide, O guide our wand'ring bark, By an-gry waves we're tossed,
2. O when threat'ning billows roll, In foamy moun-tains high,

Thy gentle hand our course must steer, O save us, or we are lost, O ev-er
Our tossing bark be-yond control, O thou be thou ev-er nigh, O leave us

near, O ev-er near, still near thee, Sweet Moth-er let us stay, Fond
not, O leave us not, mother blest, 'Lone to drift adown life's sea, O

chil-dren we will ev-er be, O turn us not a-way.
take us to those ports of rest, To stay for-e'er with thee.

No. 5. MARY QUEEN OF ALL THE FLOWERS.

Solo and Chorus.

Words by M. E. WALSH, Pupil of S. N. D.   Music by L. LAMBILLOTTE.

1. The bees are a - live in the clo - ver, Soft clouds are a - drift in the
2. The lil - y that dwelt by the wa - ter, Was breathing a song in the
3. The blossoms will glow for an hour...... In sunshine the bird-ling may

1. blue,...... The flow'rets their pe - tals un - cov - - er, The
2. morn,...... A whisper of heaven it taught her, When
3. sing,...... But fades the pale bud in the show - er, In

1. blossoms are gleaming with dew...... Sweet Ma - don -na, the
2. first her young beauty was born...... Sweet Ma - don -na, low
3. win - ter the war-bler takes wing..... Sweet Ma - don -na, re -

rit.

1. ro - ses in their glad - ness Are shedding their fragrance a - new.... Smile
2. droop - ing, in her white - ness, Un - sul - lied by shad-ow or storm,... She
3. -mem - ber when the snow- drifts, Blow cold as the win-ter they bring, . Our

1. on, there dwells no sad - ness, Where thou art gentle and true.
2. fain would seek thy bright - ness, Her fair - ness to a - dorn.
3. hearts know not De - cem - ber, For love is al - ways Spring.

Chorus.

Queen of all the flow - ers, And La - dy of the spring, . With-

- in thy own bright b ewers, . Thy ten - der - ness we sing....

No. 6. MEMORARE.

Chorus and Solo.

Words by M. E. WALSH, pupil of S. N. D.   Music by L. LAMBILLOTTE.

1. Remember, oh, remem - ber, dear - est Moth - er, Nev - er,
nev - er was it known, that a - ny sin or sor - row,
trembling in thy sun - shine, Told too oft its wail - ing
moan, Or wept un - pit - ied or a - lone.

FINE. SOLO.

1. Thro' the a - ges that are past, Thro' the
2. Thou art fair as the stars, Thou art
3. What thou wert still thou art What thou

years that lie sleep-ing, Cold and dark in the tomb of the
pure as the morn-ing, We are frail as the leaves that lie
art, be thou ev - er, O - pen wide all the gates of thy

dead long a - go, No soul ev - er came in its
low in the blast, But, ah! that sad heart nev-er
beau - ti - ful store, My life at thy feet I lay

des - - o - late weep-ing, In - vok - - ing in vain thy
sad sin-ner scorn-ing, In - vites to its re - pose the
low, thou canst nev - er Re - fuse a heart, whose throbs shall

pit - y for its woe, Thy pit - y for its woe.
fol - ly of the past, The fol - ly of the past.
pierce thine own no more, Shall pierce thine own no more.

No. 7. O HEART OF MARY.

SOLO AND DUET OR 2 PART CHORUS.

Words and Music by S. N. D.

SOLO.

1. O Heart of Ma - ry pure and fair, There
2. As some fair li - ly midst the thorns, Thou
3. O chaste a - bode of fair - est love, In
4. O mys - tic Ol - ive of the field, Which

1. is no stain in thee ; In A - dam's fall thou
2. 'mongst Eve's daugh - ters art ; Ce - les - tial pur - i -
3. thee the King re - posed ; Thou art the spouse, the
4. dost sweet balm im - part ; Thy shades from heats of

1. hast...... no share, From sin's con - trol thou'rt free. In A-dam's
2. -ty,........ a - dorns Thy crys - tal depths.chaste Heart, Ce - les- tial
3. mys - - tic dove, The fount, the gar - den closed, Thou art the
4. pas - - sion shield, And glad the wea - ry heart, Thy shades from

1. fall thou hast no share, From sin's con - trol.... thou'rt free.
2. pur - i - ty a - dorns Thy crys - tal depths, chaste Heart.
3. spouse, the mystic dove, The fount, the gar - den closed.
4. heats of passion shield, And glad the wea - ry heart.

CHORUS.

O heart.... of Ma-ry pure and fair, No beau-ty can with thine com-
-pare, From ev-'ry stain of sin thou art free, O
make us pure in heart like thee.

5.

As children to their mother flee
When storm-clouds darkly lower
||: So loving hearts will haste to thee,
In sad affliction's hour. :||

6.

As doves all innocent and pure,
Repose within their nest,
||: So we, from every ill secure,
In Mary's Heart shall rest. :||

7.

Sweet Heart, within thy depths so chaste,
We'll dwell and ne'er depart,
||: Till thou our souls hast deeply placed
In Jesus' Sacred Heart. :||

8.

And when from thy loved Heart we'll go,
To that of thy dear Son,
||: O shall we leave thee then? Ah, no,
His Heart and thine are one. :||

No. 8. OUR LADY OF THE SACRED HEART.

SOLO AND 2 PART CHORUS.

Words by pupil of N. D. San Jose.　　　　　　　　　　Music by S. N. D.

Andante espress. :8: SOLO.

1. To thee, sweet Mother, Heavenly Queen,... We
2. We call thee oft the Queen of May,.... And
3. And by this name to-day we call...... On

1. raise our lov-ing hearts to-day..... Oh, deign to lis-ten to our
2. lil - y pure, and mys - tic Rose,.. And Moth-er of our Je-sus
3. thee, by the un-wearying love,... Which thou dost for thy children

1. words, While low-ly at thy feet we pray, Oh, deign to lis-ten to our
2. dear, In whose sweet heart love brightly glows, And Moth-er of our Je-sus
3. feel, To raise our loving hearts above, Which thou dost for thy children

ri - - tar - - do.

1. words,...... While low - ly at thy feet we pray.
2. dear,........ In whose sweet heart love brightly glows.
3. feel,........ To raise our lov - ing hearts a - bove.

Sweet La - dy of the Sa - cred Heart, Be -

- fore thy shrine to - day, We kneel on earth to choose the.

ri - te - nu - to

Queen, Queen, of Heav - en's e - ter - nal May.

ri - te - nu - to

4.
Then beg of Jesus by the blood
  That flowed so freely from His Heart,
That he will bathe us from its flood.
  That chastened we may form a part.
    Cho.—Sweet Lady, &c.

5.
A beauteous, holy, loving part
  Of that much envied train and bright,
Who follow ever more the Lamb,
  Through heaven's eternal realms of light
    Cho.—Sweet Lady, &c.

6.
Then Mother, as the last May breeze
  Sighs round thy convent shrine so dear,
Assist us, intercede for us,
  That when our last sad hour draws near—
    Cho.—Sweet Lady, &c.

7.
Then, then with Jesus and with thee
  We may in love sigh life away
Into the shrine of Jesus' Heart
  As sweet as this last breeze of May,
    Cho.—Sweet Lady, &c.

MOTHER LOVED.

DUET or TWO-PART CHORUS & SOLO.

Words by S. N. D.

Music by L. LAMBILLOTTE.

f. Allegretto.

Ma - ry, hear my fer-vent prayer, Take me 'neath thy care;

O Moth - er loved, be my life, my stay, Guide and

love me, save and pro-tect me, 'Till the dawn of e - ter - nal day............

.... Ma - ry, hear my fer - vent prayer, Take me 'neath thy

care; O Moth - er loved, be my life, my stay.

"Mother Loved." Concluded.

SOLO.

1. O Moth - er loved, watch o - ver me, So help - less,
2. O Moth - er loved, watch o - ver me, From sin and
3. O Moth - er loved, watch o - ver me, When life is

1 tossed on life's rough sea; Kind - ly shed from heav - en a-
2 dan - ger keep me free; When temp - ta - tion's waves an - gry
3 bright and fair to see; Who so need thy clear guid - ing

1 -bove A Moth - er's sweet fond smile of love.
2 flow, Thy-self to me a Moth - er show.
3 ray As those that walk the flow - 'ry way.

No. 10. MARY'S TITLES.

(SOLO AND TWO PART CHORUS.)

Words by A. PROCTER.   Music by S. N. D

SOLO.

1. Thro' the world thy children raise Their pray'rs, and still we
2. Queen of heaven, when we are sad, Best so - lace of our
3. Hope of sin - ners, how ma-ny souls, Cast down by woe and
4. Ma - ry, dear - est name of all, The ho - liest and the

see, Calm are the nights and bright the days Of those who trust in thee.
pains. It tells us tho' on earth we toil, Our moth - er lives and reigns,
sin, Have learn'd thro' this dear name of thine, A pardon and peace to win.
best, The first low word that Je-sus lisped, Laid on his mother's breast.

CHORUS. *Animato. ad lib.*

Star of the sea, we kneel and pray, When tem - pests raise their

voice, Star of the sea, the hav-en reached, We call

thee, we call thee and re-joice, Star of the sea, Star of the sea.

OUR QUEEN IMMACULATE.

SOLO & TWO-PART CHORUS.

Arranged from AVE MARIA.

SOLO.

1. Oh fair - est of all vis - ions, With meek - ly fold ed hands, A-
2. Oh fair - est of all vis - ions, That met the ea - ger gaze Of
3. Ex - pec - tant yet for a - ges, That earth must yet a - wait, Fair
4. The King looked on thy beau - ty, In thy un - fall - en state, The
5. Oh fair - est of all vis - ions, En - tranc - ing mor - tal eyes; The
6. Oh fair - est of all vis - ions, Our wea - ry ex - ile o'er, In
7. We'll see thee Queen and Moth - er, Enthroned in roy - al state, In

1 -dor - ing eyes up - lift - ed, Be - fore her God she stands.
2 Pa - tri - arch and pro - phet, In far pri - me - val days.
3 Sha - ron's Rose, God's moth - er, Our Queen Im - mac - u - late.
4 Spir - it's Bride, the Vir - gin, Our Queen Im - mac - u - late.
5 veil is half up - lift - ed, We gaze in fond sur - prise.
6 thy un - cloud - ed glo - ry We'll see thee ev - er - more.
7 all thy vir - gin splen - dor, Our Queen Im - mac - u - late.

CHORUS.

Mother pure, Virgin fair, Spotless Dove, Peerless maid,

Mother pure. Virgin fair, Spotless Dove, Peerless maid, Crowned

Rall.

Queen of God's cre - a - tion, Our Queen Im - mac u - late.

No. 12. MATER ADMIRABILIS

(TWO PART SOLO AND CHORUS.)

Music arranged from CONCONE.

Moderato espress.

ƒ. CHORUS.

O Ma - ter ad - mi - ra - bi - lis, List to our fer - vent prayer, Oh, let thy lov - ing chil - - dren, Thy sweet pro - tec tion share, Thy sweet pro - tec - tion share.

Solo.

1. O Ma - ter ad - mi - ra - bi - lis, Our
2. Let an - gels swell the cho - - rus, Let
3. Be - fore her lov - - ing im - - age, 'Tis
4. O Ma - ter ad - mi - ra - bi - lis, 'Tis

1. youth - ful hearts we raise In
2. heav'n and earth pro - claim, O·
3. tru - est joy to kneel, And
4. more than rap - - turous glow That

1. soft soul - breath - ing mel - o - dy, To sing thy
2. Ma - ter ad - mi - ra - - bi - lis, The sweet - ness
3. gaze up - on the beau - - ties That faith and
4. cheers our dark and lone - some way On this sad

1. won - drous praise ....
2. of thy name ....
3. love re - veal ....
4. earth be - low ....

No. 13. STAR OF OCEAN.

TRIO AND CHORUS.

TRIO. *Allegretto,*

1. Hail thou star of o-cean, Por-tal of the sky, Ev-er
2. Oh! by Ga-briel's A-ve, Ut-tered long a-go, E-va's
3. Break the cap-tive's fet-ters, Light on blind-ness pour; All our
4. Show thy-self a Mother; Of-fer Him our sighs, Who for
5. Vir-gin of all vir-gins! To thy shel-ter take us; Gentlest

ff CHORUS.

Vir-gin Moth-er Of the Lord most high. Ev-vi-va Ma-
name re-vers-ing, 'Stablish peace be-low.
ills ex-pell-ing, Ev-'ry bliss im-plore.
us In-car-nate, Did not thee dis-pise.
of the gen-tle! Chaste and gen-tle make us.

-ri-a, Ma-ri-a Ev-vi-va, Ev-vi-va Ma-ri-a, E-

chi-la cre-a.

6 Still as on we journey,
  Help our weak endeavor;
  Till with thee and Jesus
  We rejoice for ever.—*Cho.*

7 Through the highest heaven,
  To the Almighty Three,
  Father, Son, and Spirit,
  One same glory be.—*Cho.*

THE ANNUNCIATION.

SOLO & DUET or TWO-PART CHORUS.

Words by A. PROCTER.   Music by S. N. D.

Moderato. SOLO.

1. How pure,   how frail, and white   The   snow - drops
2. For on   this   bless - ed day   She   knelt   at
3. Hail Ma - ry!   in - fant lips   Lisp   it   to-
4. Hail Ma - ry!   many a heart   Bro - ken   with

1 shine,   Gath - er   a   gar-land bright   For   Ma - ry's
2 pray'r,   When lo!   be - fore her shone   An   An - gel
3 -day,   Hail   Ma - ry! with faint smile,   The   dy - ing
4 grief,   In   that   an - gel - ic prayer   Has   found   re-

CHORUS.

Animvto.

1 shrine.   Hail Ma - ry, Hail Ma - ry, Queen of Heav'n,   Let us re-
2 fair.
3 say.
4 -lief.

-peat,   And place our snow-drop wreath,   Here   at   her feet.

No. 15. OH ! BEAUTIFUL THOU ART.

Duet.   Words by Pupil of S. N. D.

1. Oh, beau-ti-ful thou art,   Our sweet Virgin Queen,   Come reign within each
2. Oh list to strains now swelling,   E - ven to thy throne,   O call us from this
3. Ah! when we're sad and wea - ry,   Tired of life and sin,   And when the way looks

1. heart,   Peace-ful and se -rene,   See with love now thrill-ing,
2. dwell-ing,   Leave us not a - lone.   Moth-er ev - er ho - ly,
3. drear -y,   Haste thy child to win.   When death lays his fin - ger

1. All thy children's hearts,   Joy each breast is fill - ing,   Sadness now de
2. Hear us while we pray,   Vir - gin pure and low - ly,   With us ev - er
3. On our i - cy brow,   O then, near us lin - ger,   Lin - ger then as

1. -parts,   Joy each breast is fill - ing,   Sad- ness now de - parts.
2. stay,   Vir - gin pure and low - ly,   With us ev - er stay.
3. now   O then near us lin - ger,   Lin - ger then as now.

(2 PART CHORUS AND DUET.)

Andante. CHORUS.

Hail, Vir - gin, spot - less Moth - er! We come to thee to -

day.... To bring thee fair-est flow - ers And crown thee Queen of May.

DUET.

1. All hearts are now re-joic - ing, Their songs of praise a - rise To
2. Fair Na-ture crown'd with beau - ty, Now greets thee, Mother dear, Bright
3. Sweet Ma - ry, Queen of heav - en, O Vir - gin ev - er pure, Be -
3. We long to see thee Moth - er, Fain would our souls be free, Re -

CHORUS.

1. our sweet Moth-er, Ma - ry, To realms beyond the skies. Hail
2. flow - ers waft their in - cense And syl - van choirs are near.
3. -neath thy snow - y man - tle, We seek a ref-uge sure.
4. -lease the flutt-'ring cap - tives, And let them soar to thee.

D. S.

No. 17. SWEET MARY.

(SOLO AND CHORUS.)

Music by CONCONE.

Andante. ℔ SOLO.

1. As the gen - tle Spring un-clos - es, And the
2. May is Ma - ry's— she is ours— Thus the
3. Dearest Moth -er! we re - mem-ber How at
4. Take us all 'neath thy pro-tec - tion, Heart and

1. Win - ter fades a-way, Sunlight glis - tens, li - lies blow, As we
2. month is doub-ly dear; As we crown her with our flowers, Angels
3. one re - quest of thine, Je-sus at the marriage feast Changed the
4. soul and sen-ses take! Tell dear Je - sus we are thine, And He'll

1. greet the month of May. As we hail its peer-less Queen, Ma-ry,
2. glad - ly hov - er near; And the bless-ed Je - sus smiles On each
3. wa - ter in - to wine; At our feast, ah! let the flood Of our
4. bless us for thy sake; And the treasures of our Ma - ry, Up in

1. Mother of de-light, In her own es - pe - cial sea - son, Sing her
2. humble vo - ta - ry, And our hom - age to His Moth-er, Will re -
3. tears thy pit - y move, Beg, oh! beg thy Son to change it To the
4. heaven, we shall store, Naught shall steal them, naught corrode them, They shall

1. praise from morn to night.
2. - quite most graciously.
3. wine of perfect love.
4. last for ev - er - more.

Ma-ry, Moth-er sweet, Ma-ry, Mother fair, Vir - gin

Queen of May, Hear our prayer, Un-to Je-sus pray, That each day   We may

grow like thee, Our Queen of May.

No. 18. WATCH OVER US.

DUET OR 2 PART CHORUS.

Words by Pupil of N. L.

1st. V.

1. O! Moth-er loved, Our sweet de-light,
2. Be love of thee, My whole life long,

2d. V.

3. Moth - er of God, Our hope, our life,

1. One glance but cast, So fond, so bright, } Watch over us, ...
2. My sweet-est joy, My gay-est song, }

3. Sweet Moth-er, shield us in the strife. Watch over

.... Watch o-ver us, Watch o-ver us, { 1. When dark night her mantle casts, When
{ 2. Shine, then brightly, O soft star, With
{ 3. From all earth-ly toils set free, We'll

us, Watch o ver us,

1. storms and wint'ry blasts...
2. thy light driving far...
3 quick - ly fly to thee..

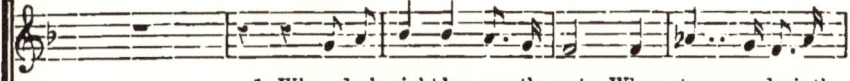

1. When dark night her mantle casts, When storms and wint'ry
2. Shine, then brightly, O soft star, With thy light driving
3. From all earth-ly toils set free, We'll quick-ly fly to

.... 1. Hide heaven's azure hue,   O ! thou star of hope shine through
.... 2. Mists that oft veil my soul,   Clouds that e'er around me roll.

1. blasts. 3. Let us rest in thy heart,   From its depth we'll ne'er depart,
2. far.
3. thee.

1. O! thou star   of hope, shine through.
2. Clouds that e'er   a - round me roll.

3. From its depth we'll ne'er de - part.

No. 19. HELP OF CHRISTIANS.

SOLO AND CHORUS.

Words by UNA.

Music by S. N. D.

Moderato.

1. O mourn - ful Moth - er,
2. Where dan - gers gath - er
3. O Moth - er of our
4. Though crowned in tri - umph

1. who didst stand Be - side the cross on Cal-vary's hill, When
2. 'round our way, And an - gry tem - pests o'er us frown, When
3. thorn-crown'd King, A mother's love we claim from thee, Thou
4. by thy Son, Queen of the heavens of end - less light, And

1. our dear Lord for sin - ners died, And na - ture's heart in awe stood
2. all the world seems dark and drear, Do thou with pity - ing eye look
3. wert bequeathed to us by Him, Our moth - er and our help to
4. list - 'ning to the hap - py songs Of ransomed souls and se - raphs

1. still. Dark days of sor-row didst thou see, There -
2. down. And be a star to light the gloom, And
3. be ; Then Help of Christians, heed our prayer And
4. bright, Yet thou art not too high to know, And

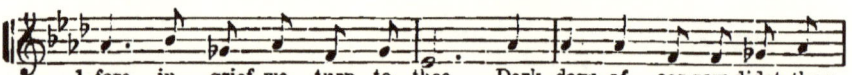

1. fore, in grief we turn to thee, Dark days of sor-row didst thou
2. guide our wand'ring footsteps home, And be a star to light the
3. guard the child-ren of thy care, Then Help of Christians, heed our
4. sym - pa - thize with hu - man woe, Yet thou art not too high to

rit - en - u - to.

1. see, There-fore in grief we turn to thee.
2. gloom, And guide our wand - 'ring foot - steps home
3. prayer, And guard the child - ren of thy care
4. know, And sym - pa - thize with hu - man woe.

O pray for us to thy dear Son, When waves of

O pray for us, O pray for us.

sor - - row o,er us roll, When dark temptations gather

When waves of sorrow o'er us roll, Oh pray for us, When dark temptations

round, Sustain and aid the fainting soul, And as we

cres -

gath-er round, Sus-tain and aid the fainting soul, And as we

cen - do.   *rit - en - u - to.*

drift o'er death's dark tide, O Help of Christians, be our guide.

No. 20. ROSE OF THE CROSS.

DUET.
Words by F. W. FABER.

Andante esp.

1. Rose of   the cross, thou mystic flower!   I   lift   my heart to
2. A wand -'rer here. thro' many_a wild,   Where few   their way can
3. Let   me   but stand where thou hast stood,   Be - side   the crimson
4. There let   me wash my sinful   soul,   And   be   from sin set
5. Be   thy   blest son my all in   all,   To   whom   for life I

1. thee:—   In   ev - 'ry mel - an - chol- y   hour,   O,
2. see:—   Bloom with   thy fragrance on thy   child ;   O,
3. tree ;   And   by   the wa - ter and the   blood,   O,
4. free ;   Drawn by   thy love, by grace made whole ;   O,
5. flee ;   And   when   be - fore His feet I   fall—   O,

1. Ma - ry ! remem - ber   me !   In   ev -   'ry mel -an - chol-y
2. Ma - ry ! remem - ber   me !   Bloom with   thy fragrance on thy
3. Ma - ry ! remem - ber   me !   And   by   the wa - ter and the
4. Ma - ry ! remem - ber   me !   Drawn by   thy love, by grace made
5. Ma - ry ! remem - ber   me !   And   when   be - fore His feet I

ritardo.

1. hour,   O,   Ma - ry !   O,   Ma - ry !   re - mem - ber   me.
2. child :   O,   Ma - ry !   O,   Ma - ry !   re - mem - ber   me.
3. blood,   O,   Ma - ry !   O,   Ma - ry !   re - mem - ber   me.
4. whole;   O,   Ma - ry !   O,   Ma - ry !   re - mem - ber   me.
5 fall—   O,   Ma - ry ?   O, .   Ma - ry !   re - mem - ber   me.

6 Lead me forever to adore
    The glorious One in Three ;
|| · And whilst I tremble more and more,
    O Mary ! remember me. :||

7 Rose of the cross, thou thornless flower
    May I thy follower be:
|| : And when temptation wields its power,
    O Mary ! remember me. . ||

ORA PRO ME.

DUET.

Words by A. PROCTER.　　　　　　　　　　　　　Music by S. N. D.

S. *Allegretto.*

1. A - ve Ma - ri - a! bright and pure,....
2. A - ve Ma - ri - a! Queen of heav'n,..
3. Then shall I, if thou, O Ma - ry,
4. When my eyes are slow - ly clos - ing,

1 Hear, O hear me when I pray;　Pains and plea - sures try the
2 Teach, O teach me to o - bey;　Lead me on thro' fierce temp-
3 Art my strong sup - port and stay,　Fear nor feel the three - fold
4 And I fade from earth a - way,　And when Death, the stern de-

ff

1 pil - grim On his long and dreary way; Fears and per - ils are a-
2 -ta - tions, Stand and meet me in the way. When I fail and faint, my
3 dan - ger Stand - ing forth in dread ar - ray; Now and ev - er shield and
4 -stroy - er, Claims my bod - y as his prey, Claims my soul, and then, sweet

espress. lento.　　　*ritardo.*

1 -round me,
2 moth - er,　Ave Ma - ri - a, bright and pure, O - ra pro me　Ora pro me.
3 guard me,
4 Ma - ry,

espress. lento　　*ritardo.*

No. 23. MOTHER OF JESUS.

(SOLO AND THREE PART CHORUS.)

Words by S. N. D.

Moderato grazia. SOLO.

Music by L. L.

1. Moth-er most ho - ly, For Je-sus sole - ly
2. Vain the en - deav or, Cold words can nev - er
3. I'm His for - ev - er, Naught shall e'er sev - er
4. Vir - gin most low - ly, Moth-er most ho - ly,

1. My heart e'er sighs, Queen of the skies, List while I
2. My love re - veal, Tell what I feel ; Christ is my
3. His Heart and mine, By links di - vine Close-ly u -
4. Thy Je - sus tell I love Him well ; Sigh-ing and

1. pray thee, Hear me, oh hear me, to thee I call !
2. treas - ure, His name is mu - sic's sweet-est flow,
3. -ni - ted, O ! Moth-er pure of fair - est love,
4. wea - ry, Dis - tant from Him and thee I pine,

1. Of - fer Him dai - ly My de - sires, my love and my all.
2. His will my pleas - ure, And His smile is sun - light's warm glow.
3. Fond-ly thus plight - ed, I a - wait our un - ion a - bove.
4. From ex-ile drear - y, O call me to thy Son di - vine.

CHORUS.

Moth-er, I pray thee, Tell, O tell Je-sus dai - ly, I love Him

much, I love Him much, Moth-er, most dear, thy voice He'll hear,

Thy sweet tones his heart will touch......

No. 23. PETITIONS TO MARY.

Solo and Chorus.

Cantabile.
Solo.

Music by L. LAMBILLOTTE.

1. Wilt thou look upon me, Mother, Thou who reignest in the skies, Wilt thou deign to cast up-
2. Wilt thou, Mother, hover ever, On my pathway still to guide? Wilt thou whisper kind di-
3. Wilt thou pray for me to Jesus, That His will I e'er may know, Wilt thou tell me then His
4. O, then Mother, I petition, And I know thy aid will come, Angels praise thee for it,

Chorus.

1. -on me, One sweet glance, from those mild eyes.   O, my Moth- er Ma- ry, still re -
2. -rection,   To the an - gel   by my side.
3. pleasure,   That I e'er may to it bow.
4. mother,   In thy ev- er - lasting home.

- member, What the sainted Ber - nard said,   None have ev - er, ever found thee

wanting, Who have called upon thy aid,   Who have called   upon thy aid.

(SOLO AND TWO PART CHORUS.)

Words from D. J. E. RANKIN'S Stabat Mater.   Music by VERSCHNEIDER.

Andante.

Doloroso

1. Stood the Mother weeping, sigh-ing, Near her Son, the cru-ci-fied,
2. Her's, what sadness and af-flic-tion, Mother of the on-ly One,
3. Who, the mor-tal without weeping, Could behold that Mother's woe,
4. For the sins of hap-less mor-tals, Scourg'd and beaten to the goal,

1. Saw him writhing, bleeding, dy-ing, Felt the sword her soul di-vide.
2. Her's, the crowned with bene-dic-tion, Je-sus dies, her glorious Son.
3. Tear-less see her, vig-ils keep-ing, Near her Je-sus suff'ring so.
4. Sees she Him at death's dark por-tals Pouring out for us His soul.

CHORUS.

Ho-ly Mother, may I bor-row, Un-measured love like thine, Grace to

ritardo

share with thee in sor-row, For Him thy Son di-vine.

No. 25. MAGNIFICAT.

Chorus and Solo.

Words by S. N. D.   Music by E. VERSCHNEIDER.

Chorus. *Allegro pomposo.*

1. Glo-ry to God! An-gel hosts are sing-ing, Is-rael's Ho-ly One

FINE.

Has for us become Ma-ry's Son, Peace on earth to us bring-ing.

Solo. *Brillante.*

1. O Mag-ni-fy the Lord, Break forth in songs my voice, In my Sav-iour a-
2. My low-li-ness He sought, On me His eyes He cast, And in me He has
3. The mighty ones he spurns, The humble he receives, Fills the soul that

grazioso.

1. -dored, My spir-it doth rejoice, While time its course shall run All ages shall pro-
2. wrought A wonder unsurpassed! His mercies to the just, From age to age he
3. yearns; The rich in want He leaves, To us for Israel's sake, His mercies still ex-

1. -claim. What God hath in me done, And bless-ed call. ...... my name.
2. shows, But humbles to the dust, His proud and haugh - - ty foes.
3. -tend, For Abram as he spake, His love shall nev - - - er end.

(CHORUS AND SOLO.)

CHORUS. *Allegretto.*

Ky-ri-e e-le-i-son, Chris-te e-le-i-son.
Pater de coe-lis De-us, Mise-re-re no-bis.

:S: SOLO.

1 Sanc-ta Ma-ri-a, Sanc-ta De-i ge-ni-trix,
2 Ma-ter......Chris-ti. Ma-ter divinae gra-ti-ae,
3 Ma-ter a-ma-bi-lis, Ma-ter ad-mi-ra-bi-lis,

O-ra, o-ra,

Sanc-ta Vir-go Vir-gi-num. Sanc-ta Vir-go Vir-gi-num,
Ma-ter in-vio-la-ta, Ma-ter in-teme-ra-ta,
Ma-ter cre-a-to-ris, Ma-ter sal-va-to-ris,

o-ra, o-ra,

f

O-ra pro no-bis, pro no-bis.

ff

o-ra, o-ra pro no-bis.

No. 27. WHO CAN WITH THEE COMPARE?

INVIOLATA, INTEGRA.

Hymn to the Blessed Virgin.

SOLO. By L. CORADI COLLIERE.

1. { Who can with thee com - pare? O Vir-gin chaste and pure ! To
   { In - vi - o - la - ta in - te - gra, Et cas - ta es, Ma - ri - a, Quae

2. { In love, in hope, ap - pear, The children of thy pain, And
   { Nos - tra ut pu - ra pec -to-ra Sint et.... cor - po - ra ! Te

rall.

1. { thee we all re - pair, Of thy protec - tion sure. Tho'
   { es ef - fec - ta ful - gi-da Coe - li, coe -li por - ta ; O

2. { call on thee to clear Their souls from loathsome stain, To
   { nunc de-vo - ta fla - gilant Cor - da et o - - ra. Tu -

1. { Queen in realms a - bove, Thou hast a Moth- er's love,.... Our
   { Ma - ter al - ma Chris-ti, O Ma - ter ca - ris - si - ma! Sus-

2. { thee the chant of praise, In grateful ac - cents raise, .. Our
   { - a.... per pre - ca - ta Dul - ci - so - - na,..... No -

p dolce.

1. { prayer, sweet Moth - er, hear, sweet Moth- er, hear, } Our
   { - ci - pe pi - a lau - - dum prae - co - ni - a, } O

2. { prayer, sweet Moth - er, hear, sweet Moth- er, hear, }
   { - bis con - ce - das ve - ni - am per sœ - cu - la. }

cal. *cal.*

D.S.

{ prayer, sweet Moth - er, hear, sweet Mother, hear.
  be - nig-na, O Re - gi - - na, Ma-ri - a.

D.S.

No. 28. EVENING HYMN.

CHORUS & DUET.

Words by M. E. Walsh.   Music by L. Lambillotte.

Andantino. **Chorus.**

Day.... is de-clin-ing,

Andantino. 2d & 3d Voices.

mf

Soon will be shin-ing All the pale stars, Ten-der-ly

beam-ing, while we are dream-ing, Watch o'er our slumbers,

ff

FINE.

pp ff pp

thou Queen of the stars. Watch o'er our slumbers, thou Queen of the stars.

pp ff pp Fine.

DUET.

1. O - pen thy heart, O ' ten - der moth - er, Hum - bly we
2. If near our dreams, dark - ness should hov - er, Cloud - ing their
3. Night clos - es round, shad - ows are fall - ing, So while the

1 kneel, breath - ing thy name, Thine is our love, ...
2 light with aught of sin, Safe in thine arms, ...
3 years pass, flow - eth time's sea, Grant us, sweet Moth - er,

1 ne'er shall an - oth er, Kin - dle be - side that ho - ly flame
2 O sweet - est Moth - er, How can that dark shade en - ter in.
3 when Death is call - ing, All our life's hopes may turn to thee.

No. 29. ASSUMPTION.

TRIO and THREE PART CHORUS.

Words AVE MARIA.

TRIO.

Music by L. L.

1. Un - fold, un - fold, ye gold - en gates of
2. Be - hold her Son de - light - ed has gone
3. Moth - er of Je - sus, hail our heaven - ly

4. Hail Ma - ry, Queen of mer - cy, grant our
5. We walk the vale of sor - row thou hast
6. Ob - tain for us thy rare hu - mil - i

1 heaven, She comes, the Queen of all the shin - ing host,— The moon be-
2 down, To meet His Moth - er, taint-less from her birth, She for - ward
3 Queen, Ten thou - sand harps swell thro' the a - zure dome, O bless - ed

4 Lord May look with pit - y on thy chil - dren here, That hum - bly
5 known, Give us from Him the grace to walk as Thou, The seed a-
6 ty, That ev' - ry act may spring from God's pure Love, Then all thy

1 -neath, her crown twelve stars of even, The sun a - bove In her great glo - ry
2 glides, while glo - ry from her crown Streams on her ex - iled chil-dren here on
3 Earth, where one so fair was seen, More bless-ed Heav'n, to which our Queen has

4 trust - ing in His ho - ly word, Our souls at last may in thy courts ap-
5 -long thy bless - ed path-way sown, Brought love - ly flow'rs, bright gar-lands for thy
6 glo - ry we may hope to see, Where He as - sumed thee in His home a-

Chorus. *Cres.*

1 lost.   The Che-ru-bim,   and Se-ra-phim,   and Heav-en's
2 earth.
3 come.

4 -pear.   The Che - rubim,   The Seraphim, and Heav-en's
5 brow.
6 -love.

hosts, now swell this glad re-frain,........... that Ma-ry loved,......... our Mother

hosts, now swell this glad refrain, this glad refrain,   that Ma-ry loved,..

Ma - ry, Queen of Heav - en shall reign, Queen of Heav - en shall reign...

Ma - ry, Queen of Heav - en shall reign, Queen of Heav - en shall reign...

rallent.

No. 30. HEAVENLY DESIRES.

DUET.

Words by S. N. D.   Music by S N. D.

1. Oh, when shall we with an - gels bright, On . gold - en harps our Moth - er
2. Oh, if 'tis now so sweet to love, And oft to breathe thy ho - ly
3. But hark! a voice from star - ry skies, Those gen - tle tones, our hearts well
4. Her children there she'll kind - ly cheer, She'll fold them in her fond em-

1 praise,   And   bask   be - neath her   smile's sweet light,   And
2 name,   What will   it   be   in   realms a - bove,   Where
3 know;   Our   moth - er loved has   heard our sighs,   She
4 -brace;   From ev - 'ry eye she'll wipe   the   tear,   And

SOLO.

1 on   her won - drous beau - ty gaze?   Sweet Moth - er, Sweet
2 Ser - aphs' ar - dor hearts in - flame? Sweet Moth - er, Sweet
3 sees us   lan - guish here be - low.   Sweet Moth - er, Sweet
4 from sad hearts all sor - row chase. Sweet Moth - er, Sweet

DUET.

1 Moth - er, Sweet Moth - er, far from heaven and thee,   We
2 Moth - er, Sweet Moth - er, soon thy sum - mons send,   On
3 Moth - er, But   no, she bids us   wait a - while,   'Mid
4 Moth - er, Sweet Moth - er, yet we'll lin - ger here,   O'er

1 lan - guish here in   ex - ile drear,   These cap - tive hearts, O Ma - ry,
2 earth no lon - ger let   us roam,   In thy bright conrts let us at
3 earth - ly scenes that pass a - way,   Then we'll be - hold her ten - der
4 life's drear waste we still will roam, And wait in hope till thou ap-

1 free   Let them   be - hold thee, Moth - er dear.
2 again, O   Ma - ry, call thy chil - dren home
3 smile, And come, with her in Heav'n to stay.
4 -pear, To guide us   to   our heav'n - ly home.

Accompaniment in "May Chimes."

DUET and SOLO.

Words AVE MARIA.

Music arranged from L'AUTOMNE by L. NIEDERMEYER.

f. Allegretto. DUET.

1. Ho - ly Jo - seph, dear - est fa - ther, To thy chil - dren's prayer in-

1 -cline, Whilst we sing thy joys and sor - rows, And the glo - ries which are

FINE. SOLO.

1 thine.

1. How to praise thee,	how to thank thee,	Bles - sed
2. Near to Je - sus,	near to Ma - ry,	And, kind
3. Sing we Jo - seph,	Spouse of Ma - ry,	And our
4. We have pray'd, and	thou hast answered,	We have
5. One more fa - vor	we will ask thee,	Thou of

1 Saint, we can - not tell,	Fa - vors count - less	hast thou
2 fa - ther, near to thee,	Keep us while on	earth we-
3 moth er's bless - ed friend,	Fa - vors count - less,	mer - cies
4 asked And thou hast given,	Need we mar - vel	Je - sus
5 all canst grant it best.	When we die be	thou still

D. C. *

1 giv - en,	Can we choose but love thee well?
2 wan - der,	And in death our help - er be.
3 constant,	Thou dost ev - er to us send.
4 tells us,	Jo - seph has the stores of heaven?
5 near us,	Bring us safe to end - less rest.

No. 32. STABAT MATER.

SOLO and TRIO or THREE-PART CHORUS.

Andante espressivo. *ff.* SOLO.

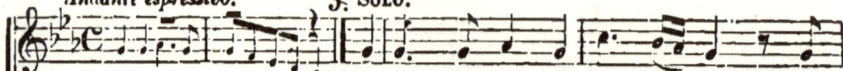

1. The Vir - gin Moth - er weep - ing stood Be-
2. Where is the man, who all unmoved, Could
3. She saw His blood pro- fuse - ly shed, For
4. O! make me tru - ly weep with thee; Mourn-
5. Let me my Saviour's suf- ferings share, And
6. May Christ's bright cross my guar - dian be, My

1 -neath the world's redeem - ing wood, Which bore her much- loved
2 see her who so tru - ly loved, Thus sunk in bit - ter
3 His own peo- ple's crimes He bled From stripes and cru - el
4 -ing with Him who died for me, Let me in grief ex-
5 His sweet cross de - vout - ly bear, For thy own Son's pure
6 Sav - iour's strength and leg - a - cy, And source of ev' - ry

1 Son, Which bore her much - loved Son; When
2 grief? Thus sunk in bit - ter grief? The
3 blows, From stripes and cru - el blows; She
4 -pire, Let me in grief ex - pire. By
5 love, For thy own Son's pure love; And
6 grace, And source of ev' - ry grace, That,

1 through her deep - ly-wound - ed breast, With sor - row's heav - iest
2 pain - ful scene who could have borne? So pure a soul with
3 saw her sweet and on - ly child, In des - o - la - tion,
4 His loved cross, with thee to stay, With thee to tread thy
5 burn - ing with love's ho - ly fire, O screen me from the
6 when my bo - dy meets de - cay, My soul may have, in

1 weight oppress'd, The sword of grief was run, The
2 an - guish torn, And none to yield re - lief? And
3 calm and mild, In life's ex - pir - ing throes, In
4 pain - ful way, Such is my fond de - sire, Such
5 venge - ful ire Of my great Judge a - bove, Of
6 that dread day, In Par - a - dise a place, In
ritardo.
Chorus.
1 sword of grief was run....... Hear then, O Moth - er,
2 none to yield re - lief?...... Hear, then, &c.
3 life's ex - pir - ing throes..... Hear, then, &c.
4 is my fond de - sire....... Hear, then, &c.
5 my great Judge a - bove....... Hear, then, &c.
6 Par - a - dise a place..... Hear, then, &c.
Source...... of love, Let me thy bitter sorrows prove, and
let me weep with thee.

SOLO and TRIO.

Words by S. N. D.   Music by F. Lowe.

Andante grazioso.   SOLO.

1. Ah! must I leave our La - dy's
2. How sweet to sing my Moth-er's
3. When I was tempt - ed, sad and
4. There from thy hand with grac -
5. Those star - ry lights so bright - ly
6. Ah! while my love to Thee I'm

1 al - tar, Where oft I've found such sweet de - light? My sad a-
2 prais - es, And breathe to her my lov - ing sighs, So fond - ly
3 tear - ful, My an - gel to thy shrine me led, Thy smile dis
4 stream - ing, Hope sweet - ly flow'd up - on my soul, Thy arms ex
5 glow - ing, Sweet Moth - er, round Thy flow' - ry shrine, Are but the
6 sing - ing, To die this hour would be so sweet, Like those sprin

1 -dieux must I now fal - ter, Must joys so pure now wing their flight?
2 on me then she gaz - es, So soft - ly beam her star - like eyes.
3 -pell'd the tem - pest fear - ful, The de - mon at thy pres - ence fled.
4 -tend - ed to me seem - ing, To woo me to thy lov'd con - trol.
5 sym - bols dim - ly show - ing The love of this fond heart of mine
6 flow'rs now per - fumes fling - ing That bloom and lan - guish at thy feet.

TRIO OR CHORUS.

Farewell, sweet month, ... , sweet month of flow'rs, ... Farewell, lov'd

Farewell, sweet month,   sweet month of flow'rs,

shrine, ... thou dear re-treat, ... But ere   have fled these happy

Farewell, lov'd shrine,   Thou dear retreat,   But ere have fled these happy

rall.   _Espressivo._

hours, ... My heart I'll leave at Ma - ry's feet, Farewell, farewell.

at Ma - ry's feet,

hours, ... My heart I'll leave   at Ma - ry's feet, Fare . . well.

D.C.

No. 34. SACRED HEART.

SOLO with TWO-PART CHORUS.

Words by of S. N. D.

From Rossini.

1. Close veiled in that sweet Sa - cra - ment, Our
2. Our Sa - cra - men - tal King un - crowned His
3. Love is not loved! O an - gels, weep, Ye
4. That heart for us could do no more, In
5. Our souls, like wea - ried doves, shall seek With-

1 Je- sus' heart, our treas - ure lies, Love's price - less, dear - est
2 sa - cred head of crowns a - bove, That our glad hearts might
3 Virgins chaste, breathe bit - ter sighs, O earth, be clothed in
4 anguish deep it sighed and bled, A cru - el spear pierced
5 -in thy Heart a sweet re - pose, Oh! in that ark them

1 tes - ta - ment, Is shrouded in that mys - tic guise; Our
2 flock a - round, And crown Him with their fond - est love; O
3 mourning deep, Withdraw your light, ye ra - diant skies; For
4 thro' its core, For us His last life's blood was shed; That
5 cap - tive keep, Our hearts with - in thine own en - close; Oh!

1 Je - sus left His realms of light, On wings of love to earth He's
2 Lov - ing Heart, Thy priceless worth, How lit - tle is it sought, or
3 all our soul's dear spouse hath died, For all His heart with love doth
4 spear, oh, Je - sus, pierced thy heart, That we with - in its depths might
5 Beau - ty an - cient, ev - er new, Thy charms a - las! too late we've

1 flown, To dwell with us 'tis his de-
2 known, Else would the bu-sy sons of
3 burn, Yet this meek Sa-viour men de-
4 flee, Oh, wound our own with love's sweet
5 known, Oh draw us now, we'll thee pur-

Solo.

1 ...ight, He makes our hearts his dear - est throne. O Sa - cred Heart, how
2 earth, Soon gath-er near that al - tar throne. O Sa - cred Heart, &c.
3 -ride, And for His love make no re-turn. O Sa - cred Heart, &c.
4 -dart, Let us ex-pire for love of thee. O Sa - cred Heart, &c.
5 -sue, These hearts would make thee all their own. O Sa - cred Heart, &c.

Chorus.

Accomp.

sweet 'twould be, If we could die for love of thee. O Sacred Heart, how sweet 'twould

rall. *ad lib.*

be, If we could die for love of thee, of thee, of .... thee.

No 35. JESUS, OUR LOVE, IS CRUCIFIED.

ƒ DUET.   DUET and THREE-PART CHORUS.   Words by FATHER FABER.

1. O! come and mourn with me a-while, See, Ma-ry calls us
2. Have we no tears to shed for Him, While sol-diers scoff and
3. Seven times He spoke, seven words of love, And all three hours His
4. Death came, and Je - sus meek - ly bow'd; His fail - ing Eyes He
5. Come, take thy stand be - neath the Cross, And let the Blood from
6. O love of God! O Sin of Man! In this dread act your

1 to her side; O! come and let us mourn with her, ...
2 Jews de - ride? Ah! look how pa - tient - ly .... He hangs; ....
3 si - lence cried For mer - cy on the souls of men ;—....
4 strove to guide With mind - ful love to Ma - ry's face ;—....
5 out that side, Fall gent - ly on thee drop by drop ;—....
6 strength is tried; And vic - to - ry re - mains with love, ...

p CHORUS.

12345 Je - sus, our Love, is cru - ci - fied. Je - sus, our Love, is
6 For He, our Love, is cru - ci - fied. Je - sus, &c.

cru - cified, Jesus, our Love, is cru - cified.

And. espressivo. *f* SOLO.　　SOLO and TWO-PART CHORUS.　　Pupil of S. N. D.

1. Mys-t'ry of love, to thee we turn, . . . As o-cean waves un-to the
2. Food of our souls, without thine aid . . . With toils o'er-la-den we must
3. Up-on our hearts O! lay thy hand, . . Its sa-ving touch will cure each
4. Pas-tor of souls, who lead'st thy flock . . In fields of flow'rs with per-fume

1 moon . . . And drink from flow-ing streams that burn . . . . With-in thy-
2 die, ... E'en as the sum-mer flow-ers fade, ... When win-try
3 ill, ... Dread storms are quelled at thy com-mand, . . . Then bid our
4 sweet, . . . And mov'st a-side the thorn and rock, ... That might re-

CHORUS.

1 -self, O Heav-en's boon, O Heaven's boon;　　Mag-net of hearts, our souls are
2 blasts are sweep-ing by, Are sweeping by.　　Thou giv'st un-to the wea-ry,
3 pas-sions, peace, be still, Peace, be still.　　O, Cure of souls, we turn to
4 -tard the stumbling feet, The stumbling feet:　　To bring them where the streamlets

1 thine, . . O'erflow them with thy love di-vine.
2 rest, . . . And still'st the ach-ing of each breast.　} Sweet Sa-crament, boon from a-
3 thee, . . . Say but one word, our ills shall flee.
4 flow, . . . To bask se-cure in love's bright glow.

-bove, In-flame our hearts . . . with darts of love, with darts of love.

5 Lover of souls! that fondly guardest
　The heart from earth's affection free,
And with the bliss of heaven rewardest
　The heart that beats ‖: alone for thee: ‖
O, never let another dwell,
　Within this breast thou lovest so well.
　　　Sweet, &c.

6 O, bread of Angels! Food of love!
　That fill'st the heart with sweetest bliss,
Thou art the rarest boon above,
　And what has earth ‖: compared to this ‖
O, without thee the soul is dead,
　Thou art its Life, Celestial Bread.
　　　Sweet, &c.

No. 37. COMMUNION HYMN.

Words by S. N. D.   **SOLO and TWO-PART CHORUS.**   Music by S. N. D.

Andante espress. SOLO.

1. I am my Love's, and He is mine,   O, Earth at - tend, ye Heavens
2. Lo! Je - sus, tender friend most true,   With love un - tiring stands and
3. From sin - ful wand'rings I return;   No more, no more from thee to
4. I've found Him whom my soul doth love,   I'll hold Him fast nor let Him
5. Close lock'd with-in His fond embrace,   His Sa- cred Heart reclines on
6. When life is o'er, to me He'll say,   "A - rise, my love, the winter's

1 hear!   Your migh - ty Lord, your King di - vine ...... Is
2 knocks,   The drops of night His head be - dew, ... And
3 roam,   Thy con - trite child, oh, do not spurn, ... Sweet
4 go,   I've naught but Him in heaven a - bove, ... He
5 mine,   Its throbbings flood my soul with grace, ... And
6 past,   The rains have ceas'd, come, haste a - way, ... Heaven's

1 now my bosom's guest most dear;   Be - hold the vast Cre - a - tor
2 glit - ter 'mongst His drooping locks;   He speaks — my love, thy heart un-
3 Je - sus, take the wand'rer home;   Ye an - gels all, re - joice in
4 is my all in all be - low;   Lo! an - gels near me hov - er
5 raptur - ous love and bliss di - vine;   My love to me, and I to
6 end - less day has dawn'd at last;"   In raptur - ous love then face to

1 makes   His home with - in His creature's breast,   His
2 -close,   And let thy Je - sus come there - in,   With-
3 heav'n,   A sin - ner weeps, the lost is found!   The
4 'round,   From open - ing skies bright legions dart,   For-
5 Him,   Who feed - eth 'mongst the lil - ies pure,   By
6 face,   My Je - sus all unveiled I'll see,   Up-

rallentando.

1 realms of ......glo - ry He for - sakes,   'Tis in   my heart He   loves to
2 -in its ....depths I would re - pose,   I'm wea - ry   of these   days of
3 robe and .... ring, the kiss are given,   God's pard'ning love   a   soul has
4 Je - sus, ... their dear King they've found, With - in   the heav - en   of   my
5 crys - tal .... streamlet's mar- gin dim,   In deep - est shades and haunts ob-
6 -on His .... Heart, in His em - brace,   I'll sweet- ly   rest   e - ter - nal

CHORUS.

1 rest.   My Dear - est Lord, my love, I'm   thine,...... And
2 sin.   My Dear - est Lord, &c.
3 crowned.   My Dear - est Lord, &c.
4 heart.   My Dear - est Lord, &c.
5 -scure.   My Dear - est Lord, &c.
6 -ly.   My Dear - est Lord, &c.

thou, my Je - sus, art all mine,   My heart for - ev - er Thine shall

rit.

be,........   O! keep it,   Je - sus,   all   for   Thee.

No. 38. HYMN FOR THE RELIGIOUS PROFESSION.

SOLO and TWO-PART CHORUS.

Words by S. N. D.

Music by C. von Weber.

And. espress. Solo.

1. Go ye forth,........ O Si - on's daugh - ters, See your
2. Come from Her - mon's dew - y moun - tain, Prince's
3. For the Spouse 'mongst lil - ies feed - ing, Home and
4. Pov - er - ty,.......... my on - ly treas - ure, For my

1. King .... in bright ar - ray, Je - sus crowned in His es-
2. daugh - ter, spot - less dove, Gar - den closed and sealed-up
3. friends,........ from you I part, He in sol - - itude me
4. share.......... I've chos - en thee, Lord, Thy will...... is all my

1. -pous - als, Joy - ful is His heart to - day;
2. foun - tain,' Thou hast won thy Je - sus' love;
3. lead - ing, Sweet - ly speaks un - to my heart;
4. pleas - ure, O - be - dient un - to death I'll be;

1. Come to - day, O Spouse to Si - on, From the leopard's heights a-
2. On thy brow thy Je - sus pla - ces, Lil - ied crowns of chas-ti-
3. Not on Thabor's mountain on - ly, Where I taste such joys to-
4. World, false world, a - dieu for - ev - er, I re - nounce your vaunted

1. -round, ... From Li - ba - nus ...... and dens of li ons,
2. -ty, ... He decks thy soul........ with price - less gra ces,
3. -day, ... But on Cal - v'ry's sum - mit lone ly,
4. charms, ... Earth and Hell........ com - bined can nev er,

ritardo. CHORUS. *con anima.*

1. Haste, to - day thou shalt be crowned. I'm thine, my Je - sus, thine for-
2. Robes it with His pu - ri - ty. I'm thine, &c.
3. With my Je - sus will I stay. I'm thine, &c.
4. Tear me from my Je - sus' arms. I'm thine, &c.

-ev - er, O precious chains, thrice ho - ly vows, From the world..my heart ye

D.C.

sev - er, And bind me to my Heav'nly Spouse. FINE.

ST. ALOYSIUS.

DUET & CHORUS.

Music by L. LAMBILLOTTE.

Allegro grazioso.

1. O thou, on whose bright na - tal day Wast giv'n to
2. O thou who a crown cast a - way To be with
3. May tho't, word and deed be from sin As far as
4. Thy war - fare is past and a - way; Re - cede the

1 Ma - ry's ten - der care,...... And who, be - neath her lov - ing,
2 Christ des - pised and poor,...... Teach me to walk thy pure and
3 thine, as chastely free,...... That we from Ma - ry's ten - der
4 clouds that dark'n earth's skies,...... For thee has dawned the hap - py,

1 gen - tle sway, Kept thy soul like to hers as fair.
2 hum - ble way, Hap - py still, tho' but small our store. } Sweet flow'r of
3 heart may win All the love that it gave to thee.
4 hap - py day, The bright heav -ens glad sur -prise.)

love, that sought to bloom unknown, A Saint, 'mid gaudy pomp and worldly pride.

CHORUS.
Angel - ic youth, blest Al - o - y - sius, Guide thou our
Angel - ic youth, blest Al - o - y - sius,
hearts thro' sin's dark tide, Angelic youth, blest Alo-
Guide thou our hearts thro' sin's dark tide. Angelic youth,
ff
-y - sius, Guide thou our hearts thro' sin's dark tide, Guide thou our hearts thro sin's dark
blest Al - o - y- sius, thro' sin's dark tide, Guide thou our hearts thro' sin's dark
ff
tide.
tide.
D.S. 𝄋

No. 40. BLESSED SACRAMENT.

SOLO and TWO-PART CHORUS.

Words by FATHER FABER.

Solo. *Moderato religioso.*

1. Je - sus, my Lord, my God, my all,.... How can I love Thee as I
2. Had I but Ma - ry's sin - less heart,.. To love Thee with, my dearest
3. Oh, see! with - in a creature's hand.. The vast Cre - a - tor deigns to
4. What hap - pi - ness can e - qual mine?.. I've found the ob - ject of my
5. He chose my heart for His a - bode, .. He there be - comes my dai - ly

1. ought, And how revere this wondrous gift, So far surpass- ing hope or thought.
2. King, O with what bursts of fervent praise, Thy goodness, Jesus, would I sing.
3. be, Re-pos-ing in - fant-like, as though, On Joseph's arm, or Mary's knee.
4. love, My Je- sus dear, my King di - vine, Is come to me from heav'n above.
5. bread, There on me flows His healing blood, There with His flesh my soul is fed.

CHORUS.

Sweet Sa - crament! - we thee a - dore! .. Oh, make us love thee more and

more; Sweet Sacrament! we thee a - dore! Oh, make us love thee more and more.

6 Ye angels, lend your heav'nly tongues;
   Come, and with me in praises join;
   Come, and unite in thankful songs,
   Your sweet, immortal voice to mine.

7 O, that I had your burning hearts,
   To love my God, my spouse most dear!
   O, that He would, with flaming darts,
   Raise in my heart a heav'nly fire!

8 Dear Jesus! now my heart is Thine;
   O, may it from Thee never fly!
   Hold it with chains of love divine,
   Make it be Thine eternally.

9 Vain objects! that seduced my soul,
   I now despise your fleeting charms;
   In vain temptation's billows roll,
   I lie secure in Jesus' arms.

DUET and SOLO.

Words by Mrs. MONROE.

Music by S. N. D.

DUET. *Moderato espress.*

1. O list, my loved an - gel, As - sent to my vow, And ac-
2. In in - no-cence keep me, And watch the bright flow'r,
3. My light be 'mid dark - ness, Mine aid thro' the day, And
4. Be near me, and round me Thy bright presence fling, My
5. O guide me, bless'd an - gel, To heav - en and God, In the

SOLO.

1. -cept...... this young heart,.... That is of - fer'd thee now. My
2. pure...... let it bloom,....Un - til life's...... clos-ing hour! In the
3. ev - er in prayer,..Teach me what...... I shall say; Then
4. heart.... close en - fold .... With thy pure,...... snow- y wing. 'Neath
5. straight,.. nar - row path...... The child Je - sus hath trod; His

espress.   *cres.*

1. Moth - er's soft eyes...... beam with ten - d'rest light,...... As I
2. heart .... of my Moth - er let mine find re - pose,...... Like a
3. Ma - ry will smile .... as she lists to thee, ... And
4. Ma - ry's bright man - tle thou may'st ev - er stay, ... O
5. Moth - er watched Him...... with such ten - der care, ... O

1. kneel.... and in - voke.... thy pro - tec - tion this night.
2. dew - drop en - shrin'd.. in the heart...... of a rose.
3. grant.... the pe - ti tion thou'st prof - fer'd for me.
4. keep .... me there with .... thee, sweet an - gel, I pray.
5. ask......her to take .... me to dwell.. with Him there.

No. 42. OUR LADY OF THE SACRED HEART.

Words and Music by Sisters o.'Notre Dame.

1. Sweet
2. Sweet
3. Sweet
4. Swee'

Andante espressivo.

dolce.

1 La - dy of the Sa - cred Heart, Thy peer- less vir - gin charms Woo'd
2 La - dy of the Sa - cred Heart, What joy thy bo -som fill'd, When
3 La - dy of the Sa - cred Heart, From Je - sus' o - pen'd side, On
4 La - dy of the Sa - cred Heart, Pro - claim thy pow'r a - bove, From

1 Je - sus from His heav'nly throne, To rest with-in thine arms. Woo'd
2 close to thine Thy In-fant's heart, In gen - tle pul- ses thrill'd. When
3 thee the wa - ter and the blood, Flow'd as a sav- ing tide. On
4 Je - sus' wounds send pierc-ing darts, Trans - fix our souls with love. From

Used by permission of JOHN CHURCH & Co.

1 Je - sus from His heav'nly throne, To rest with - in thine arms.
2 close to thine thy In -fant's heart, In gen - tle pul - ses thrilled.
3 thee the wa - ter and the blood, Flow'd as a sav - ing tide.
4 Je - sus' wounds send pierc-ing darts. Trans - fix our souls with love.

CHORUS.

Adagio espressivo.

1st VOICE.

Sweet Lady, Sweet Lady, Sweet Lady of the Sa-cred Heart.

2d VOICE.

Sweet Lady, Sweet Lady, Sweet Lady of the Sa-cred Heart.

3d VOICE.

5

Sweet Lady of the Sacred Heart,
  When Death, with icy hand,
‖: Lays on our frighted hearts his touch,
  O Mary, near us stand ! ‖

6

Sweet Lady of the Sacred Heart,
  If thou wilt hover near,
‖: Death's deepest shades in thy clear light,
  Will quickly disappear. :‖

www.ingramcontent.com/pod-product-compliance
Lightning Source LLC
Chambersburg PA
CBHW030716110426
42739CB00030B/658